W9-DET-556

A special gift for

_____

with love

_____

date

_____

Stories, sayings, and scriptures to Encourage and Inspire

hugs™

for
Daughters
from Dad

HOWARD BOOKS
A DIVISION OF SIMON & SCHUSTER
NEW YORK   LONDON   TORONTO   SIDNEY

DAVID OWEN

Personalized Scriptures by
LEANN WEISS

Our purpose at Howard Books is to:
•*Increase faith* in the hearts of growing Christians
•*Inspire holiness* in the lives of believers
•*Instill hope* in the hearts of struggling people everywhere

Because He's coming again!

Published by Howard Books, a division of Simon & Schuster
1230 Avenue of the Americas, New York, NY 10020

Hugs for Daughters from Dads © 2006 David Owen

ISBN 13: 978-1-58229-566-4
ISBN 10:   1-58229-566-2

10   9   8   7   6   5   4   3   2   1

HOWARD is a registered trademark of Simon & Schuster, Inc.

Manufactured in the United States of America

For information regarding special discounts for bulk purchases, please contact Simon & Schuster Special Sales at 1-800-456-6798 or business@simonandschuster.com.

Paraphrased scriptures © 2006 LeAnn Weiss
3006 Brandywine Dr., Orlando, FL 32806; 407-898-4410
Edited by Between the Lines
Cover design by Stephanie D. Walker
Interior design by Tennille Paden
Photography by Chrys Howard

To my daughter, Jenna.
You are the reason I was able to write this.
You've taught me more than you'll ever know.
You taught me to love and live in a way that
I never could have without you.
Without you, I would not be complete.
Love, Dad

Contents

Chapter One

Teacher

Chapter One

Teacher

I'm your fountain of life. I light
your way. I'll instruct you and
teach you in the way you should
go. I'll counsel you and watch
over you. You're a teacher too . . .
passing on what you've learned
to your children and to their
children's children.

LOVE,

Your God of All Wisdom

—from Psalms 36:9; 32:8; Deuteronomy 4:9

We dads love to teach our daughters. We teach them things we know and enjoy, like fishing, football, golf, bike riding, gardening, or carpentry, because we want to share something we love with someone we love. But we dads also teach our daughters about things we'd never even thought about before they were born—things like ballet, horses, baking, music, cats, and tea parties.

We teach our daughters because we love them so much. We want to prepare them for the future, help them succeed, and protect them from disappointment, so we teach them what we think they'll need to make it in life. But did you know that daughters teach dads too?

Every dad has his eyes opened a little wider at the

birth of his daughter. Daughters change everything—for the better. You've changed me for the better—beginning with your first tiny smile. You taught me about wonder the first time your little hands reached out to touch my whiskered face. You taught me compassion every time you hurt. You taught me about humility when I tried to bathe you as a newborn and when I learned to change your diapers.

But daughters usually teach their dads the most during their teen years, when they get a lot smarter than their dads. They teach their dads about the swift passage of time and the importance of living fully every moment. Most of all, daughters teach dads about life—its wonder, its value, its promise, and its blessing.

You have been a wonderful, patient teacher. Thanks.

Our lives are connected by a thousand invisible threads, and along these sympathetic fibers, our actions run as causes and return to us as results.

Herman Melville

Kinsey was beautiful and smart and perfect. Jim studied his daughter's profile, his emotions suddenly difficult to control.

Life Lessons

The massive silver SUV stopped near the door of the red-roofed hotel on Fordham Avenue. Jim Thomas turned off the engine but left the keys dangling from the ignition while his wife, Becky, swung open the door and grabbed her purse. "Guard our stuff," she told him, pushing the lock to secure the entire vehicle. "Be right back." She jumped down and closed the door behind her with a thud.

Jim thought it sounded different than usual—muffled. He glanced into his rearview mirror at the cargo filling every available crevice and couldn't help but chuckle to himself. The real surprise was that they could get the doors closed at all, not that their shutting sounded muffled.

But the chuckle was gone in an instant—replaced with an unexpected stab in his heart as he remembered what the packed gear represented. Tomorrow he would deliver precious cargo to the big university—his eighteen-year-old daughter, Kinsey. He didn't want to do it. He wondered if he really could.

Kinsey's head popped up in the backseat. She rubbed her

sleepy eyes, yawned, and looked around curiously. "Are we there?"

She looked like a little girl waking up from a nap. It caught Jim off guard, disarming him. Was she really old enough for college? To be away from him? He studied her thoughtfully in the mirror. "Almost," he answered softly, hoping his voice wouldn't betray his unexpected emotions. "Your mother went in to get the key."

Kinsey was beautiful . . . and smart . . . and perfect. Pride welled up like a wave that threatened to overcome Jim. He tried to rationalize his strong emotions that were suddenly difficult to control. This wasn't like him. *It must be the late hour. I'm overly tired.* It had been a long day. It was almost two o'clock in the morning, and he had driven for hours after working all day.

Jim studied his daughter's profile as she stared out the window. *What's she thinking?* he wondered. She'd seemed so excited about going to college. Was it starting to hit her now—as it was hitting him—that this would be the end of a special time they had shared? That he'd soon be saying good-bye to his little girl and hello to a young woman he hadn't expected would come nearly so soon?

It started to rain, sporadically at first, then harder. The sound was soothing, and the water spotting the windows and running down the glass cast weird shadows from the hotel's lights.

She must be sleepy, Jim guessed at the reason for her stillness.

Rain always had a hypnotic effect on him too. Although her hair was dark, like his, her face reminded him of Becky's when they'd first met. Why, she hadn't been much older than Kinsey was now. The thought startled him.

"Dad?" He almost missed Kinsey's quiet question.

"Yeah?"

"I'm not sure I'm ready for this."

"You'll do great," he said gently.

Kinsey's voice dropped even lower. "How do you know?"

"You're smart. You're a hard worker, and you learn fast. You'll make lots of good friends. You're gonna love it."

"I like things the way they are now," Kinsey said, her words coming faster. "I have everything figured out. I know what to expect. I have my friends—and you and Mom. I know the best place to buy jeans or get a burger. I don't know anything about college. What if it's not as good as what I'm saying good-bye to?"

"You already know more than I did at your age," he told her simply. "You've figured out that life brings changes we can't anticipate or control. But then I've always known you were smart. You've been teaching me about life since the day you were born."

"What?" Kinsey leaned over into the front seat. "You're the wisest man I know. You've always been the one teaching me—to tie my shoes, to ride a bike, to play basketball—algebra, money, politics . . . boys . . . What could I possibly have taught you about life?"

Jim could still feel the raw emotion of that very first lesson.

The tiny silver car stopped beside a red hotel on Connecticut Avenue.

"Yes!" twenty-five-year-old Jim exulted, the one happy voice in a chorus of pained and sympathetic groans. "That's mine! I own it!" Jim glanced gleefully at his deed while his friend Bill thumbed dejectedly through his dwindling cash. "With a hotel, that'll cost you six hundred dollars—enough to buy me another hotel. Thanks a lot, buddy!"

As Bill counted out the Monopoly money and handed it over begrudgingly, Jim proudly positioned the new hotel he got from the banker, Bill's wife, Sue. As Jim's own wife, Becky, strained to reach across her pregnant belly and roll the dice Jim happily counted his fat wad of colorful currency. He liked to win, and he usually did. He was proud of his competitive and aggressive nature—proud of where it had gotten him so early in life.

Jim's life was exactly as he had anticipated it would be. He and Becky were expecting their first child soon. Jim couldn't wait. He was ready for the joys—and increased costs—of fatherhood. He and his best friend, Steve, had recently started a construction company, and it was doing well. They'd already sold two homes and had just signed a deal to custom-build a large house. Even now Steve was on his way back from checking out some promising property that just might launch their first development project. *Like Monopoly*, he thought. He was good at putting up houses. The company's financial future—and his own—looked bright. He'd be able to give this baby everything he hadn't had as a child.

Jim glanced at his watch. Where *was* Steve? *He'll be bummed that he missed the game.*

The phone rang. Sue, the hostess, finished counting out two hundred dollars to Becky for passing Go, then hurried to answer the phone.

"That's probably Steve," Jim called after her. "He'd better have a good excuse for being so late."

It was Sue's turn, so the game stopped as they waited for her return. For some reason the silence seemed awkward.

"It's Steve . . ." Something in Sue's voice sounded an alarm in Jim's head. When he looked at her face, it only confirmed his fears. Grim disbelief soon melted into grief and tears.

"That was Steve's wife," Sue told the somber group as she hung up the phone. "There's been an accident. They've taken him to the hospital. He's . . . not expected to live."

Jim sat in the hospital waiting room, his face buried in his hands. His cheeks felt almost sticky. For the first time in his life, he was crying in a public place without embarrassment. How could this be happening? How could Steve be dead? What would happen to their business now? He chided himself for being selfish. What did it matter? Steve was dead. But it did matter, especially with the baby coming—*now!*

The stress and trauma of Steve's unexpected death had sent Becky into labor—right there at the hospital. While his friends comforted Steve's widow, Jim grappled alone with his sorrow and fears. It wasn't supposed to happen like this. He was supposed to be in the delivery room, not out here waiting for news about his breech baby and his wife's emergency C-section. His best friend was dead, maybe his business too, and now this crisis with Becky and the baby.

As he waited for news, Jim felt overwhelmed by the fragility of life. Death was real, even for the young and strong, like Steve— or Becky. For the first time he truly feared that something bad might happen to Becky or the baby. How could he handle it? His feeling of control over life had been an illusion—an illusion that was being irreparably shattered. He fervently wished everything were like it had been yesterday, before he knew this awful truth of life—and death.

He was startled out of his dark thoughts by a nurse in surgical garb. Jim watched anxiously as she lowered her mask to reveal a face that . . . yes, he could breathe again. Her relaxed smile was all the message he needed. "You have a beautiful little girl, Mr. Thomas, and your wife is doing well."

Jim knew he would never forget the first time he held Kinsey. His calloused hands trembled as he reached to take her. She was as bald as a bowling ball. Her tiny ears were smashed to the sides of her head from her awkward position in the womb, and she was screaming with all her strength. "It's OK," he whispered, and she seemed to hear him. She stopped crying and lay calmly in her father's hands.

And suddenly Jim knew that it truly was OK. In that one moment, life had eclipsed death. Yes, he had lost much, but he had gained even more. Life was precious. This new little life was proof.

The days that followed were crazy for Jim with a new baby, a recovering wife, and an emotional funeral for a friend. During that week of tragedy and blessing, Jim found himself standing for hours, staring at Kinsey through the window of the hospital nursery. "No one will take her," his father-in-law gently teased him. "You don't have to stand guard."

But Jim knew that he wasn't guarding Kinsey; he was guarding himself, guarding his heart. In the midst of death and sorrow, Jim desperately needed to see life. And that's what he saw when he looked through the window at his little girl—life, hope, and promise. Jim realized he had been taking life for granted—something he vowed never to do again. Every time he looked at Kinsey, he would be reminded of God's blessings, the miracle of life, and the promise of the future.

Kinsey slumped back into her seat as Jim finished telling his story. "Wow!"

Father and daughter were silent. "Life is precious, Kinsey," Jim said fervently. "Don't take it for granted or get too comfortable. Life is about change. Your life is changing now; so is mine. But we've got to embrace it and move bravely ahead." Jim saw Becky emerge from the hotel. She started to shield her hair from the rain with her purse, then stopped. She turned her head toward the heavens and let the rain splash on her face for a moment before racing for the car.

"Life is good," Jim summarized. "That's what you taught me."

Chapter Two
Encounter

Chapter Two

Encourager

Make encouraging and building
up each other a daily habit.
Cheer on the timid, help the
weak, and practice patience with
everyone. Remember that I
am for you. You can achieve
far beyond your human limits
because I strengthen you.

ENCOURAGING YOU,

Your God of Hope

—from Hebrews 10:24; 1 Thessalonians 5:14;
Romans 8:31; Philippians 4:13

Do you remember the words your dad shouted when he was helping you learn to ride a bike? Maybe he said, "You're doing great!" or "Keep trying" or "Thatagirl!" The words don't really matter; just the fact that he was there was encouragement enough. Dads have plenty of opportunities to encourage daughters to set worthy goals and take pride when they meet those goals.

Dads encourage daughters even when they make mistakes. Maybe you didn't put much effort into a school project and got a bad grade, but Dad was there to say, "Next time you'll be more prepared." That's no one's favorite kind of encouragement, but expecting daughters to do their best is one way dads help them achieve their goals.

And then, like magic, something changes. Most daughters are seventeen or eighteen before their dads begin to understand what's happening, but the first signs often show up at age thirteen or fourteen—that's when daughters start making mature decisions, decisions that make dads proud.

And then it's your turn—you become your dad's encourager. He's been there for dance recitals and ball games with encouraging words. Now you encourage him—by the way you've grown and become responsible, by the good decisions you make, and by the life you live. Even when you don't know you're doing it, your encouragement makes life better by bringing joy to your father's heart.

What lies behind
us and what
lies before us
are tiny matters
compared to what
lies within us.

William Morrow

Bob's eyes met his daughter's, and for a moment he forgot to breathe. That expression of hurt and disappointment always tore at his heart. He desperately wanted to say the right thing.

Jumping Forward

Bob's perfectly raked pit of sand erupted as his seventeen-year-old daughter, Callie, landed her final jump. "Mark it," shouted the official working the triple-jump event. Callie stood, dusting the loose sand from her legs and arms and kicking the grass to clean the sand from her shoes. She didn't wait to hear the measurement. Bob could tell by her posture that she knew it hadn't been enough. She bit her bottom lip and seemed to fight back tears as she walked over to the equipment bag she'd left by the football goalpost.

It was hard for Bob to stand in his usual place, rake in hand, when his overwhelming urge was to go to Callie and comfort her. He had hoped and prayed all day that she would do better. It broke his heart to see her so discouraged. He willed himself to look away from Callie and rake the sand for the next jumper. He'd raked the pit for every home track meet since Callie was in junior high.

This was the final meet before the big district competition, and Bob could feel the excitement in the air. All the contestants were fine-tuning their techniques, getting ready for next week's meet, which would determine who would advance to the state competition. It was a beautiful day at Eagle Stadium, but in Bob's mind everything was overshadowed by Callie's struggles.

Bob was proud of Callie's accomplishments: She had excelled in track, showing marked improvement each of her first three years in high school. Last year she won district, was named outstanding field performer in the district meet, and qualified for the state competition in long jump and triple jump. The only way she could improve this year, her last, would be to win at the state meet. Their small hometown newspaper wasn't the only one to predict a great senior year for Callie: papers across the state heralded her as the athlete their local favorites would have to beat.

Bob was keenly aware of how heavily the pressure of people's expectations weighed on his daughter. But he also knew that most of all Callie felt the pressure of her own hopes and dreams. She had committed herself wholeheartedly to winning, and he was afraid that nothing but winning would be enough for her.

But this year hadn't gone according to plan. Early in the season Callie had pulled a muscle. The injury had limited her practice time and thrown her off stride. Months later she still hadn't reached the level at which she'd performed the previous year. Bob desperately wanted to wrap his arms around his daughter and say just the right thing to make things better.

Hold on for just one more jumper, he told himself. *One more and you're through.*

Bob mechanically finished his assignment, then hurried to put away the rake. As he walked toward Callie, who was sitting dejectedly in the grass, he said a silent prayer. *God, give me the words to encourage her.*

He sat beside Callie and took a deep breath. She didn't look up but stared glumly at the ground, head in her hands.

"Hey," he said softly. "You OK?"

"Hey, Dad," she acknowledged him, slowly lifting her head. "I'm OK, just disappointed." Bob's eyes met his daughter's, and for a moment he forgot to breathe. He'd seen that look a hundred times before—big brown eyes and one big tear rolling slowly down her beautiful cheek—but it still had the same effect on him. It was the look she'd had when her puppy died, when her friends made fun of her in junior high, and when the guy she was sure would ask her to the prom asked someone else. That expression of hurt and disappointment always tore at his heart.

He wanted to be strong for her, so he tried to keep his voice calm and upbeat. "You did better than last week, and you're getting there. Try to look at this positively."

"But Dad," Callie protested, "I almost got beaten by a sophomore. Next week is the district meet. If I don't jump way better than this, I won't even place." She didn't pause for breath as she spilled her frustration and disappointment. "This was supposed to be my year, the year I could win a state title. But now I might not even make it past district. All that hard work for nothing."

Bob allowed an awkward moment of silence as he thought carefully how to respond. He desperately wanted to say the right thing. "You think you've worked hard for nothing?" he probed calmly. "I know you're disappointed that things haven't gone better, but never think that you've worked hard for nothing."

Callie bit her lip and looked at the ground again as Bob continued. "Callie, when you were just a skinny little seventh grader and you announced that you were going to run track, I didn't know whether to laugh or cry. I thought it was just another thing you'd give up in a month when you got bored. I wanted to laugh, because you'd never shown even the slightest interest in or aptitude for anything athletic."

"Why'd you want to cry?" Callie looked at him curiously.

He chuckled. "Because I'd heard how boring track meets were."

Callie laughed with him, giving Bob courage to continue. "But I've got to admit, Callie, you surprised and impressed me. I loved watching you compete. For me it wasn't about winning or losing; it was about the look of confidence on your face and how you'd throw yourself in the sand, straining for just one more inch. I learned that you had a lot of ability and the determination to do a good job. After only a few meets, I was addicted."

"But Dad . . . what's that got to do with today?"

"Well, you never would have been here today without the confidence you've gained over the years—and I wasn't the only one who noticed your potential. Remember when Coach Mash asked you every day before freshman season if you were going to run varsity track? He recognized your talent and gave you an opportunity to compete at the next level. Don't you think that was worth something?"

"Yeah, I guess." Callie still sounded unconvinced.

"And I'll never forget the district meet in your freshman year. Mom and I would have been excited if you had just managed to place. But going into the triple-jump finals, you were in the lead!"

Callie wrinkled her nose. "I lost by just a quarter of an inch."

"Ah, yes, to your teammate Molly—a senior. But your performance, for a freshman, was outstanding."

"Wow, you remember," Callie sounded pleased. "I like to hear you tell it, Dad," she admitted with a shy smile.

Bob felt warm inside. He was making progress. "Everyone who watched you jump that day knew you had a bright future on the track team."

"I thought I did too." Callie sniffled. "But then this year . . ."

"Callie, don't give up now. You didn't give up when you hurt your knee running hurdles. You came back that year and went to regional competition in triple jump. Remember how good it was to come back and succeed? Remember how you felt when the coaches from other teams all knew your name? You won their respect. That's something nobody can take from you."

Callie sat silently for a moment and then slowly straightened her back. "I know you're right, Dad. Thanks for reminding me." She started to get up, but Bob gently grabbed her hand.

"Wait just a minute." He took a deep breath. "You know, Callie, you may not do as well as you did last year. With the pulled muscle, you haven't been able to practice as much. Last year was special. Everything was clicking, and you were healthy, strong, and full of confidence."

His eyes locked with Callie's as he continued. "But do you remember what it was like away from the track, at home? We weren't getting along very well. Maybe, as I watched you growing up, I was scared I'd lose my baby girl. Maybe you were exploring your growing independence. But we fought all the time—you started getting into trouble, and I was always mad about something.

"Yet we got past all that, and we like being together again. Who knows," Bob ventured tentatively, "maybe it's even because you've struggled on the field." He talked faster in response to Callie's surprised expression. "I've been so impressed at the way you've handled disappointment. You've never given up, even when going on was difficult and painful. You've really matured this year. I like who you've become.

"Don't get me wrong," he assured her. "Nobody wants you to succeed more than I do. But I wouldn't trade the way our relationship has grown for anything—not even a state championship. As far as I'm concerned, this has been our best year yet."

Bob fell silent as he tried to decipher Callie's reaction. Her brow was furrowed, but he suspected she was thinking, not upset. Still, it felt unsettling not being able to read more.

"Bob . . . there you are." Coach Mash was approaching, ending the father-daughter moment. "Can you help time the relays?"

"Sure. Be there in a minute."

Bob grunted as he unfolded his legs and stood. He grabbed Callie's hand and pulled her to her feet, then hugged her. "You've got a week to practice. Just do your best. That's all you can do. Now go find your friends and have some fun. I love you."

"Love you too," Callie said, giving her dad another hug. "See you at home."

Bob's thoughts were still full of Callie as he walked to his car after the meet. How much of what he'd said had she really heard? He had wanted to encourage her and make her feel better, but the older she got, the more helpless he felt.

As he slid behind the steering wheel and put his key into the ignition, he was startled to hear the passenger door open and see Callie slide into the seat beside him.

"What's wrong?" Bob asked. "I thought you were going out."

"Maybe later, Dad. I've got to do something important first."

"Like what?"

"Like telling you that . . . well, what you said before . . . you're right. This has been a much better year for us. And if I had to choose, I'd take a good relationship with you over a championship—hands down." She leaned over and kissed Bob lightly on the cheek. "Thanks for encouraging me and . . . well . . . being my dad."

Stunned, Bob couldn't find his voice until Callie was out of the car and slamming the door. His fingers still worked, so he pushed the button to open the passenger window and leaned over to call after Callie. But she was already gone. What did he expect? She was a track star, after all.

He relaxed against the car seat. "Thank *you*," he said quietly, "for encouraging *me*."

Suddenly Bob knew everything would be OK. He still believed Callie was going to win the state competition, but it really didn't matter anymore. His daughter was already a winner, and he couldn't be more proud.

Chapter Three

Guardia

Chapter Three

Guardian

I pass on My love to you and
My righteousness to the upright
in heart. Continue to live in Me.
Be rooted and built up. I'll
strengthen you in faith and make
you overflow with thankfulness.
My plans stand firm forever,
and the purposes of My heart
continue through all generations.

HELPING YOU SHINE BRIGHTLY FOR ME,

Your God of Light

—from Psalm 36:10; Colossians 2:6–7;
Psalm 33:11

Every day is full of opportunities to make a difference in somebody's life. Some we ignore or don't even notice; others we take full advantage of. The resulting impact is especially true with dads and daughters. You have made a profound difference in my life. Perhaps what I treasure most are the opportunities just to spend time with you. When you were young, we spent lots of time together making memories —treasures that will be ours forever.

Opportunities are gifts from God, gifts we can choose either to use or discard. As we've both grown older, I've learned to cherish the opportunities we've enjoyed together. Each one was a chance to invest in each other and in the future. And now, as you grow stronger and wiser and make the most of your God-given potential, I better understand the importance of having taken advantage of those opportunities. Each moment we shared, each memory we forged together, sowed seeds that have grown and blossomed with the passing of time.

When I look at you and the beautiful person you are even still becoming, it pleases and reassures me to know that I am a part of you forever. Even if my mind grows cloudy with age and my earthly body wears out and dies, I know that you carry me— the memories, the shared times, the essence of who I am—in your heart.

When saving for
old age, be sure
to put away a few
pleasant thoughts.

Author Unknown

"Karen'll be here," Hardy protested. Even so, he glanced anxiously at the clock. What could be keeping her?

The Life Preserver

The blue sky, warm sun, and shimmering lake melted unnervingly into a cold, sterile hospital room as Hardy's dream evaporated. The weight that had been his youngest daughter, Karen, pressing against his chest in an excited hug was transformed into the heaviness of pneumonia in his lungs, and the sputtering sound of the outboard motor on his small fishing boat turned out to be only his roommate, Clarence, hacking uncontrollably. Disconsolate at the loss of his beautiful dream, Hardy Stevens rolled onto his left side, away from Clarence's coughing fit. He wondered if he might be able to recapture the dream—and his youth, now long gone—if he went right back to sleep. But it was not to be.

"Awake?" Clarence sounded hopeful.

Hardy considered ignoring his roommate; a suspicion flitted through his mind that Clarence had awakened him purposely. But compassion for the lonely, cantankerous man in the next bed overcame Hardy's self-protective desire for solitude. He sighed. "Yes, Clarence, I'm awake. What do you want?"

"It's almost two-thirty. I told you . . . she's not coming."

Hardy put on his glasses so he could read the extra-large numbers on the clock from home that his wife, Marge, had placed on the credenza next to his hospital bed. "It's not even two-twenty," Hardy protested. "Karen'll be here."

With his glasses on, he could see Clarence shaking his head knowingly. "You'll see. This is always how it starts. At first they come because they feel guilty if they don't. But the longer you're in here, the less you'll see of your kids. My kids ain't even come see me at all this time." He snorted derisively. "All my money's used up for doctor bills. I got nothing left to give 'em, so I ain't likely to see 'em back."

"I'm sorry for you." Hardy managed to stay civil in spite of the sudden grumpy hostility he felt. "But my kids aren't like that. Angela and Brian come on weekends; Karen's right here in town, so she comes every day."

"It won't last." Clarence sounded annoyingly sure of himself. "We're old—we're yesterday's news. They don't need us anymore. The more time passes, the less we have to do with our kids' lives and the less they even think of us at all. You'll see I'm right."

An icy chill pierced Hardy's heart. Perhaps Clarence's constant pessimism had caused his own deeply hidden fear to surface. He didn't want to be a burden to his kids. Most of all, he didn't want to be irrelevant to their lives. As he grew older and his health declined, would that be his defining legacy to his children and grandchildren—the sick old man who always needed something?

"No, *you'll* see," Hardy said forcefully, perhaps trying to convince himself more than Clarence. "Karen's coming." Even so, he glanced anxiously at the clock. *Two twenty-three. What could be keeping her?* She was usually punctual—just like her dad. He consciously pushed away his concern that maybe, just maybe, Clarence's lonely plight would become his own sorry fate.

He was startled—and then relieved—by the loud knock on the hospital-room door. And then, without waiting for an answer to her knock, Karen burst into the room. Instantly Hardy felt better—stronger, invigorated. He always did when she was around.

"Pap, you're looking better today, not so pale. How are you feeling?" She tested the temperature of his forehead with her wrist and then kissed it sweetly. She pulled yesterday's flowers from the vase by his bedside and replaced them with a fragrant bouquet of fresh flowers—from her own garden, Hardy knew.

"Hello, Mr. Washington," Karen greeted Clarence, producing a small cut-glass vase and another handful of beautiful, fresh blooms for him. "I see you're sitting up. Feeling better today, are you?"

He harrumphed grumpily in response, but she bent and kissed his furrowed brow anyway, and then she turned to place the flowers on the empty credenza by his bed. Behind her back Hardy was pretty sure he saw a smile light up Clarence's face—it was the first he'd seen in days.

"How much longer are they going to keep you here, Pap?

Have you seen the doctor yet today? What did he say? When did he say it would be OK for us to go fishing again? Did you eat lunch yet? What'd you have? Is there anything you want or need?"

Hardy chuckled and raised his hands in a gesture of surrender. "Slow down, Bani!" he pleaded. Bani was a pet name he'd given her as a child because she was spunky and full of energy, like the little "banty" chickens he'd raised in his youth—the name still fit her more than forty years later. "Yes, I saw the doctor this morning," Hardy reported. "He said I might be able to go home in a few days, but it'll be a few weeks before I'll be well enough to fish our favorite spot again."

"Harrumph." Clarence wrinkled his nose disdainfully. "Girls don't fish."

"This one does," Hardy responded proudly. "She's more of a fisherman than her older brother, and my favorite fishing partner since the first time I took her out."

"I was six," Karen announced proudly. "I'll never forget that first fishing trip. It was the best day I could remember. I was so proud that you let me go along with you—just the two of us. I felt very special."

"You were special," Hardy remembered with a chuckle. "I'll never forget that day either."

"I caught a big fish the first time I dropped my line in the water. I was ecstatic that I'd caught a fish before you did."

"Well, sure you did." Hardy defended his fishing honor. "I

got you set up first and hadn't even cast my line yet. B'sides, I'd taken you to the Honey Hole—the spot so great that you'd have to be sleeping not to catch a fish." He winked at Karen and smiled, a mischievous gleam in his eye. "I really had you going there."

"Aw, you did not," Karen protested as she adjusted Hardy's pillow to support his head more comfortably. "I knew you were teasing me all along."

"I saw the look on your face," Hardy countered. "You were scared."

"I was just scared we wouldn't be able to find the Honey Hole again."

"You were scared I was going to leave you on that stump."

"Honey holes . . . stumps . . . abandoning six-year-old children . . . you people make less sense than a politician without a speechwriter," Clarence grumbled.

"Here, Clarence," Karen proposed. "Tell us what you think."

Clarence rolled his eyes as Karen started the story.

"We'd only been fishing a short while when we ran out of bait. That's because we were catching so many fish."

"And because you kept losing your bait," Hardy interjected. "But this little gal loved fishing so much, she didn't want to quit. She pleaded with me to be able to return once we got some more bait."

"But Pap said he wasn't sure we'd be able to find the spot again, so he suggested leaving me sitting perched on a nearby stump while he went to get the bait—so he'd recognize the spot when he came back again."

"Told her I'd only be gone a few minutes and that I hadn't seen any alligators that morning, so I was pretty sure she'd be fine." Hardy laughed out loud. "Bani got the same wide-eyed look as the crappies we were catching and did some mighty fast thinking to make sure I wouldn't be leaving her on that stump."

Clarence raised his eyebrows in a quizzical expression.

"I suggested we put an extra life preserver on the stump instead of me as a marker," Karen explained.

"And so we did," Hardy announced with satisfaction. "It was a very smart idea for such a little girl." He lowered his voice as he confessed: "I hope it's not because I scared you silly that you still remember that day."

"Oh, Pap," Karen rubbed his shoulders consolingly. "I knew you wouldn't really leave me. You were my protector, my lifesaver. You wouldn't even start the car until all of us kids were buckled up. You wouldn't let me set foot in the boat until my life preserver was fastened securely. I knew you'd never just abandon me on a stump in the middle of the lake."

Hardy grasped Karen's soft, delicate hands and squeezed gently, hoping his grip somehow would communicate the love and pride that filled his heart. Karen squeezed back and smiled and then pulled her hand from his with a start.

"Oh, that reminds me . . ." She dug in her purse, finally

producing her wallet stuffed full of receipts and coupons. "Here, Clarence, you can see what we're talking about." She held a photo at arm's length from Clarence, mindful of his old, farsighted eyes.

Clarence studied the photo for a moment and then harrumphed again.

"What is it?" Hardy asked, curious.

"The picture of the life preserver on that old stump at the Honey Hole," Karen said matter-of-factly.

Hardy's mind tingled with surprise and wonder. "Let me see that."

Karen brought it dutifully to her father's bedside and let him hold it.

"You have a picture of this?" he asked incredulously. "But how? We didn't have a camera with us that day."

Karen smiled, a mischievous twinkle in her eye. "Flip it over and look at the next picture, Pap," Karen urged him gently.

He did and instantly understood: there was a picture of Karen's youngest son, eight-year-old Jaden, perched, smiling, on the stump wrapped in the orange life vest.

"We go there a lot." Karen seemed surprised at his surprise. "Lots of good family heritage and history at that spot, and it's still a honey hole."

"You told Jaden the story?"

Karen laughed. "Only a million times. He loves that story. It was his idea to re-create the scene and take some pictures.

I thought sure I showed you these last summer. I hope you don't feel bad that I didn't."

Hardy shook his head wordlessly. His chest felt somehow lighter as it seemed that his heart might float away and burst with pride and joy. He didn't feel bad, he felt wonderful—relieved, renewed, reborn. Clarence was wrong. He could embrace, not fear, the future. For no matter how old, how feeble, or how useless he felt, much of him would live on: healthy, young, and vibrant. Karen would keep the stories, the family heritage—and him—alive and well for the next generation.

Hardy knew he'd found the Honey Hole again.

Chapter Four

Inspiration

Chapter Four

Inspiration

Inspire each other to love and good deeds. Love in action is life-changing. Love extends patience and kindness. It sets aside pride. Love counters selfishness. It gives you the ability to forgive when you've been hurt. Love celebrates the truth. May your love always protect, always trust, always hope, and never give up on people. Real love never fails and is the greatest gift.

INSPIRING YOU,

Your Source of Love

—from Hebrews 10:24; 1 Corinthians 13:4–8

Before I was your father, I was just a man. An ordinary man with ordinary dreams and aspirations—a man with flaws, warts, and blind spots. I never thought of myself as being better than any other man. But when you entered my life, everything changed.

Suddenly, being ordinary wasn't enough. I wanted to be more than that. You inspired such love in my heart that I would have climbed mountains for you, sacrificed anything to provide for you, and given you the moon or anything else you wanted—as far as it was in my power. This feeling manifested itself in my playing dolls with you, selling your fund-raising cookies at my office, driving two hours to watch you compete, helping you with your homework, looking in on you while you slept, or praying at your bedside.

Being your father is part of what defines me. It makes me so much better than I was before. Personal ambition, power, pleasure, and wealth— their appeal to me has paled in the light of your radiant love for me and mine for you.

You inspire me to be the best—the best father I can be. I like who you inspire me to be. I know I'm not perfect, but you've never asked me to be. And the truth is, I'm much better with you than I ever was without you. You deserve the best, and I'll do everything in my power to be the best for you.

We are all
failures—at least,
the best of us are.

J. M. Barrie

You only thought I was sleeping when you used to come in here begging God—and me—to forgive you.

Shadows

The hinge on the cabinet door seemed to squeak a little louder than usual as Ted Brooks reached for his favorite coffee mug. The whole house was eerily quiet; against the engulfing silence, every sound seemed to be amplified. He could even hear the last few drops of coffee falling into the coffee pot. It wasn't unusual for Ted to be the first one up. He liked getting an early start, and he usually had lots to do. But today was different. Today his oldest daughter, Nicole, was getting married.

The whole week had been hectic. Each family member's schedule had been full, capped off by the wedding rehearsal the night before. Ted was glad to have a little time to just relax. He poured himself a mug of coffee and then walked quietly down the hall toward the den.

But he stopped suddenly when he found himself face to face with Nicole—or rather, her picture. Photographs of his parents, his brother and sisters, and his children lined the hallway of his small country home. He had walked by the pictures a thousand times and rarely paid them any attention, but this morning was different. The photos of Nicole seemed to jump out at him, drawing him to carefully study each one. He stared at the picture of his little girl at her kindergarten graduation and couldn't suppress a huge smile at her toothless grin and obvious excitement. But his joy was tinged with sadness and regret.

He stood alone in the dimly lit hallway, his eyes moving slowly from picture to picture, his mind flooding with memories. The chubby elementary-school girl gave way to the awkward junior higher; then to a cheerleader striking a confident pose in her uniform; and finally to a beautiful, poised high-school graduate. Soon a new picture of Nicole would grace the wall—her wedding photo. The thought both pleased and frightened him. How had it all happened so quickly? Why had he squandered so many opportunities to spend precious time with his daughter? Emotions overwhelmed him as he looked again at the snaggle-toothed little kindergarten girl with curly, blond pigtails. *How can it be?* Warm tears stung his eyes and threatened to overflow. His little girl couldn't possibly be all grown up and ready to start a family of her own.

Startled by the sound of a door opening, he turned the other way, not wanting anyone to see him so emotional.

"Ted?" It was Janet, his wife. "What are you doing?"

"Just having a cup of coffee," he answered, doing his best to keep his voice from cracking.

"Why are you up so early?"

"You know me—can't sleep past five," he said with a laugh, trying to hide the real feelings in his heart.

"You're crazy!" she said with a sleepy chuckle as she ducked back into the master bedroom. "I'm going back to bed. It's going to be a long day, so I want to sleep as long as I can."

"OK, hon. I'll cook breakfast when you get up." Ted was glad to be alone with his thoughts again.

Staring quietly back at the wall of memories, he drank his last sip of coffee and started back to the kitchen to refill his mug. As he walked past the door of Nicole's bedroom, he suddenly felt a powerful urge to look in on her one last time.

He quietly opened the door just a crack and peered inside. The beam of light from the hallway illuminated her sleeping face, reassuring him that he hadn't disturbed her. His body cast a long, shapeless shadow across her sleeping form. He opened the door wider and walked quietly into the room, closing the door behind him. As his eyes adjusted to the darkness, he was able to make out the features of Nicole's face. What a beautiful young woman she had become. His heart filled with pride and gratitude.

He felt compelled to kneel beside Nicole's bed and talk to God once again. *God, thank You for Nicole,* he prayed silently. *Thank You for giving me a second chance.*

When he looked up, he was startled to realize Nicole was looking at him.

"Just like old times, eh, Dad?" It was more of a statement than a question.

"Not *just* like old times." Ted smiled ruefully. "Apparently you don't remember what those old times were like."

"Sure I do," Nicole countered gently. "You only thought I was sleeping when you used to come in here begging God—and me—to forgive you."

"You knew?" Ted was genuinely surprised. "Why didn't you let me know you were awake?"

"If you wanted me to know, why didn't you come in when you thought I was awake?"

"Probably because I was never sober when you were awake," Ted admitted, still humiliated by the truth.

"You were never sober when I was asleep either." Nicole still managed to sound kind.

"I couldn't face you." Ted covered his face with his hands. "Somehow it felt safer to really face myself and talk about it in the darkness."

"Like now."

"Nicole, I haven't been a very good father—"

"Stop," Nicole said forcefully, taking his hand in hers. "You're a great father, and you know it."

"I've gotten better." Ted squeezed his daughter's hand. "But for the first half of your life, I wasn't worthy to be your father. You deserved so much better."

Nicole smiled consolingly. "I never wanted any father but you."

"How can that be?" Ted asked incredulously. "Don't you remember the miserable father I was? I never was there for you—or for anyone else in this family. The drugs and alcohol consumed me. They stole my time and my devotion. They destroyed my health, our finances, and our family. You couldn't even play summer-league soccer because I used your uniform money to get high. I couldn't function unless I was high or drunk. Who'd even want a father like that to show up for your school programs and T-ball games?"

"I did," Nicole whispered.

Ted looked his daughter in the eye. "I know." He ran his hand roughly through his thinning hair. "I know, and I never understood it. No matter how many times I broke my promises to you, no matter how often I disappointed you, you never stopped wanting me around, never stopped believing I'd be there the next time. What's a drunk supposed to do when his own little girl won't give up on him but keeps expecting the best of him—even believes him when he says he'll quit?"

Nicole sat up and leaned toward him with intensity. "But you did quit, Daddy." She hadn't called him that in years. "And it took great courage and strength to turn your life around. I can't even imagine how you had the strength to do such a thing."

"Do you want to know how I did it?" Ted asked her. He could see her curiosity as she nodded. The room grew silent in an expectant pause. Ted licked his lips and chose his words carefully. It was important that he say this right.

"I did it for you, Nicole, and in the strength of your belief in me."

He could see her eyes grow round, and then she threw herself against his chest. He held her close and continued. "I wanted to be the father you deserved—the father you believed I was—or at least the father I could be. You inspired me to change." Tears were running freely down his cheeks and into his beard and Nicole's hair. "You made me want to be a better father."

"Oh, Daddy, I never knew." Nicole's voice was muffled, her face still buried in his chest.

"Thank you, Nicole, for giving me back my life. Thank you for giving me back my self-respect. I like the person you believed I could be, but I wouldn't have been able to be that person without your help and inspiration. But most importantly, thank you for giving me a second chance with you. It still pains me that I messed up so much of your childhood. I look at the photos in the hallway and am reminded of how much I missed. But I'm also thankful for the good years we've had more recently."

Ted let out a long breath. "Now you're getting married and leaving home . . ."

Nicole pulled away and looked up at him, shaking her head and opening her mouth to protest.

"It's OK," he assured her, pressing a finger to her lips to quiet her. "I don't see this as an ending, just another new beginning. Jeff is a good man, and I know he'll make a good husband—and father. I'm happy for you and so proud of my wonderful, grown-up, almost-married daughter. And if you'll let me," Ted teased with a smile, "I still plan to be in the picture. Think that would be OK?"

With a twinkle in her eye, Nicole squeezed his hands and kissed his cheek.

"I *do*!"

Chapter Five

Friend

Chapter Five

Friend

Grow in faith, goodness, knowledge, self-control, perseverance, godliness, kindness, and love. If you continue growing in these areas, you won't be ineffective or unproductive in things that really count. Your faith pleases Me. When you earnestly seek Me, I'll reward you.

Loving you always,
Your Heavenly Father and Friend

—from 2 Peter 1:5–8; Hebrews 11:6

What is a friend? A friend is someone we like having around. We look forward to seeing friends, think what they say is clever, and laugh—or groan—at their jokes. When a friend is having a difficult time, our hearts ache for that person. We'd do anything in our power to help make things better.

Being a friend is about sharing the same vision and heart, not about sharing the same appearance or demographics. But sometimes friends even share the same genes and the same address. And sometimes, when you're very blessed, you find that one of your very best friends is your own daughter.

I guess I'm blessed. Not only do I have the best daughter I ever could have imagined, but I also have the best friend I could want.

I'd rather be with you than with just about anyone else. You brighten my day, make me stand taller, delight my father's heart, and wow me just by being who you are.

Our relationship is no longer defined by loose teeth, learning to drive, or curfews. We've gone way beyond that. I love to know what you're thinking, what makes you happy or sad, your hopes and dreams, and what makes you who you are. I guess I just love feeling close to you.

I hope you'll think of me as your friend too, because I promise to be there when you need me. I'll celebrate your successes, share your joys, help you up when you stumble, and stand in your corner no matter what life brings—just like a good friend should.

Blessed is the influence of one true, loving human soul on another.

George Eliot

Lauren's tough, quiet father seemed to be struggling to keep from crying. That realization brought a flood of emotion and tears to her own eyes.

Amigos

A white Mazda Miata turned right off the service road and quickly into the parking lot of Amigos Restaurante. The small sports car looked out of place in the lot that was full of work trucks equipped with the tools of various trades. Pulling into a parking space, Lauren Webb hardly noticed anymore that hers was the only "car" in the lot. She turned off the ignition and jumped from the car, shutting the door behind her and pressing the remote lock on her key ring. She heard the familiar *beep beep* that told her the car was securely locked.

She waved to her dad, who stood on the walkway by the front door of the diner. "Hey, Dad!" Lauren yelled, trying to make herself heard over the eighteen-wheeler that raced by on the interstate behind her. "How did you beat me here?"

He winked at her. "I know a shortcut."

"As slow as you drive, it must be a really good shortcut," Lauren teased. She stepped up onto the sidewalk. "I had to go back in the house and get my Spanish book. I have my final tomorrow and need to study between classes. I am so ready to be through taking tests."

"You're almost done," her dad said, opening the door for her. "Just a few more days and you can leave high school behind for good."

They sat down at the same booth they'd shared for years and were greeted by the familiar voice of Rosa, the waitress. "Here's your coffee, Ron. You want the usual, huevos rancheros?" Lauren's dad nodded, and Rosa turned her attention to Lauren. "And what'll you have this morning, hon?"

"Just a glass of orange juice," Lauren answered. "I'm not too hungry today." She tried to analyze the strange feeling that was dulling her hunger. She didn't feel sick. Excited, maybe? Stressed? Maybe even a little nostalgic. Hmm. She'd have to sort out these feelings later.

"So I guess this is our last Thursday breakfast at Amigos," her dad said as he stirred cream into his coffee. He didn't look at her, and he seemed almost nervous.

The realization sank in slowly for Lauren. "It is, isn't it?" With the frantic pace of end-of-the-year school tasks and preparing for graduation, she hadn't allowed herself to truly grapple with the prospect of saying good-bye to her weekly breakfast out with her dad. Finally acknowledging that it was the end of an era brought the confusing feelings she'd been having bursting to the surface. Yes, now it made sense: she felt wistful—sad—like she was giving up something precious.

"I wish I could tell you how much I've enjoyed our breakfasts together," her father said, head down, into his coffee. "And how much I'm going to miss them . . . how much I'll miss *you*."

Lauren was shocked to hear his voice crack. She studied him closely to try to determine if something was in his throat or if he was struggling with his emotions. Yes, it was true. Her tough, quiet father who usually found it so difficult to speak of his feelings seemed to be struggling to maintain control and keep from crying. She realized with wonder that he felt very strongly about what he was saying. The realization brought a flood of emotion and tears to her own eyes.

"Thanks, Dad." She reached out and put her hand on top of his rough, calloused workman's hand. "I'll miss my time with you too," she admitted. "But don't make me cry! My eyes will get all red and puffy, and I've got to take pictures with my friends this morning."

Her dad laughed and looked into her eyes for the first time that morning. "You're a nice girl, but you sure do cry a lot," he teased her. It was what her kindergarten teacher had said about Lauren when she first started school.

"Yeah, I used to think I took after Mom, but now I realize I get that from you!" Lauren teased back.

He squeezed Lauren's hand and smiled. "I guess I should be thankful you were such a crier. If you hadn't been, we probably would've missed out on all this."

"Maybe I had it planned all along," Lauren suggested mysteriously.

Her dad snorted. "Yeah, right. No five-year-old girl could

pretend that well. I never saw so many tears or heard such a ruckus over just going to school in the morning."

"Little girls know how to get their daddies to do what they want," Lauren insisted.

"And you always did have me wrapped around your little finger," her dad acknowledged. "But no one's that good. You were miserable!"

"I was," Lauren admitted ruefully. "I couldn't understand why you and Mom would just leave me there—in a strange place with strangers. I wanted so badly to go home with you . . . to my own toys and house, where everything was familiar and safe."

"Every day was a battle just to get you into the school," her dad shook his head at the memory. "And then your teacher said you cried or sniffled most of the day. You wouldn't play with the other children, didn't even want to take your jacket or rain boots off."

"That was so I'd be ready to go home—just in case you came and got me."

"One day I had to do some work at the school, and I saw you on the playground and waved. Your teacher asked me not to let you see me next time I was there, because you cried the rest of the day."

Lauren laughed. "I know it. Back then it just felt like school was eternal. If only I'd known how quickly it would all fly by." The thought made her feel wistful again, but she pushed the emotions aside and returned to the lightness of their shared memories. "So is that why you started taking me to breakfast . . . to bribe me not to cry?"

"More or less," her dad admitted, removing his cap and scratching his head. "Your mom and I were at our wits' end. Didn't know how to help you. And your mom read in a book how important a father is to a daughter's self-esteem and ability to separate from the mother and be independent."

"So you were elected to try to talk some sense into me?"

"More like try to figure out what was wrong and how we could help. I took you to your favorite place for breakfast—"

"Amigos!"

"Just the two of us. We talked about what you didn't like about school, then tried to focus on what you thought you might like. We discussed some of the girls who might make good friends and how to get to be friends. We also talked about how to handle the one kid who was picking on you."

"Oh, Chuckie Olson," Lauren groaned at the memory.

"That's right, Chuckie."

"I remember feeling so important and grown-up being invited to breakfast with you without Mom. I felt special. And I also remember that after breakfast, when you drove me to school in your big ol' work truck, I felt big and strong. You encouraged me to be strong at school and told me I had nothing to worry about. Then you promised me that you or Mom would always be there for me when I got home. It made me feel safe and protected."

"Your teacher said you didn't cry a bit that day." Her dad

still seemed proud at the memory. "So that's when we made our deal—you wouldn't cry at school anymore, and we'd go to breakfast together every Thursday morning before school."

"Did you ever expect it to last so many years?" Lauren asked.

"No," he admitted, fidgeting again. "But I sure am glad it did."

"Lauren . . ." Suddenly he was serious and earnest, his eyes holding hers with an intensity that surprised her. "I don't have the words to tell you what our time together has meant to me, but maybe this'll make it clear."

He produced a card from between the layers of his shirts. It was a graduation card. She read the words on the front aloud: "'For my special friend as you graduate from high school.' Did they run out of daughter cards?" she asked lamely, unsure how to handle her father's emotion.

"No," he said plainly. "Mom and I will give you one of those at your party. This one's just from me. It says exactly how I feel about you every Thursday morning. Read it."

Curious, she opened the card and read silently:

When I first met you, I never imagined that we'd be friends; but I'm so glad we are. Being your friend is one of the best parts about being me. Always remember that although you leave much behind, you'll never leave behind my friendship. I'm proud of your accomplishment. But mostly I'm proud that you're my friend.

It was signed, "Love always, Dad."

Before she could speak, her dad produced a tiny package from his shirt pocket and pushed it across the table to her. "Open it."

Her fingers trembled as she tried to slide off the ribbon and rip open the shiny purple paper. It was a ring box, and inside was a beautiful set of three rings.

"It's a friendship ring," her dad explained as she took them out and tried them on. Two of the rings featured delicate, beautiful silver hands that interlocked when worn together. The third ring—the middle one—featured a heart that was hidden by the two hands. She slid the set on her finger. It fit perfectly.

"Oh, Dad," she squealed breathlessly. "I love it. I'll cherish it always. Thank you." She leaned across the table and kissed his cheek.

"Huevos rancheros and orange juice." The waitress placed their food between them. "What a beautiful ring!"

"Isn't it?" Lauren held it out proudly. "Oh, Rosa, wait a minute." She dug in her purse, pulled out a camera, turned it on, and handed it to the waitress. Then she got up and slid onto the seat beside her dad. She leaned against him, striking a pose. "Take our picture, will you?" she pleaded. "It's the end of school, and I want a picture of me and my friend."

Chapter Six

Example

Chapter Six

Example

You are My workmanship, purposely created in Me to accomplish things I've prepared you to do. May Christ be your model. You're never too young to set an example through your speech, your life, your love, your faith, and your purity. Focus on things that make an eternal difference instead of worrying about earthly things.

SETTING YOUR PERSPECTIVE,

Your Faithful God

—from Ephesians 2:10; 1 Corinthians 11:1–2;
1 Timothy 4:12; Colossians 3:2

Sometimes life seems too complicated when you're a dad. We like to think we're strong, responsible, and self-reliant. We often believe that we can or should fix anything that's not quite what it should be. We want everything to be perfect for our families, and we feel it's up to us to make it that way.

We're keenly aware of the need to be good examples to our daughters. We want to guide you, through our actions, to be mature, responsible, well grounded, hard working, self-confident, and capable of handling whatever life might send your way. Sometimes that causes us to be so wrapped up in the many details of what we're trying to accomplish that we lose sight of the big picture. That's when you surprise us by cutting through the morass with your clear, sweet vision of life as it truly is and life as it could be. Such revelations come to dads through their daughters: life's not about the cacophony, but the quiet; families are for loving, not lecturing; joy can be found in any circumstance; people are more important than presents.

You've taught me all this and more. Mostly I've learned by watching your example. Your quiet strength, your sense of fun and fairness, your ability to adjust and roll with the punches, and your predisposition to see the good in everyone—these are the ways I want to be like you, daughter. Thanks for your example!

The people who influence us are those who have stood unconsciously for the right thing; they are like the stars and the lilies, and the joy of God flows through them all the time.

Oswald Chambers

Willie was gratified to see a little face straining to look at him through the front window. She disappeared, and he knew she was running to the door to greet him. For the first time all day, he felt like running too.

Silent Night

Willie groaned as he climbed down from his dusty old Silverado work truck. He wasn't even thirty, but he felt more like an old man lately—stiff, sore, and exhausted. Working outside in the cold weather and keeping up with the extra holiday rush orders was wearing on him physically, but the added demands of Christmas were also wearing on him emotionally. As much as he had looked forward to being done with work for the day, he still dreaded what would face him at home: in-laws.

Slamming the truck door shut, he took a deep breath and braced himself to go inside. Bekah's mother and three younger sisters had been staying with them in their three-bedroom house for less than a week, but it felt more like a month. Willie liked his in-laws, he really did, and he was dogged by guilt for the way he was feeling, but they just didn't have room for so many people and all their stuff. And those folks had a lot of stuff! It seemed there was no place in the house that Willie could go to escape the clutter and noise and just be alone.

On top of that, this would be the first Christmas since Bekah's father had left her mother for a woman Bekah's age, so it was an especially stressful time for the entire family. Almost every night Bekah and her family had stayed up talking and crying into the early hours of the morning. Instead of festive and joyful, the mood in the house always felt sad. And he missed Bekah. It seemed her father's betrayal had caused her to question the reliability of marriage—even their own. It hurt Willie and made him feel like an outsider in his own home. With the financial stress of purchasing their first house added to the mix, it was no wonder he hadn't been sleeping well.

Glancing at the house, Willie was gratified to see a little face straining to look at him through the front window. He couldn't help but smile when his little girl started jumping up and down in excitement once he looked her direction. She disappeared, and he knew she was running to the door to greet him. For the first time all day, he felt like running too.

"Daddy!" shrieked the sweetest four-year-old in the world, embracing his leg in the tightest hug she could muster.

"Katy-kins!" Willie sang back to her, lifting her into his sore and weary arms and kissing her forehead.

"You're home, you're home! Mommy said you'd take me to McDonald's when you got home."

Willie laughed and tousled Katy's hair as he set her back on the floor. "Mommy said that? Well, it must be so, 'cuz Mommy's pretty smart." He gave Bekah a quick kiss on the cheek as she came around the corner. "What's up?" he asked softly as Katy ran to get a drawing to show him.

"Same old thing. Mom's having a tough time. I just thought maybe you could use a break and would enjoy spending a little fun time with Katy."

"Mmmm, sounds great," Willie admitted. "Just let me grab a quick shower, and we'll be on our way. Oh, and thanks."

Willie had hoped to be able to relax as he sat in a booth watching Katy play on the climbing toys, but instead, he felt himself growing more tense. Too many children populated the room, and all of them were older and larger than Katy. He was afraid she'd get hurt, and it was difficult to keep track of her this way. He eyed Katy's half-eaten hamburger and contemplated finishing it. Too excited to eat, she had promised to come back and eat a few more bites after playing for a while. But now it was cold, and he doubted she'd touch it. Although he still wasn't full, like a good dad, he decided to leave it for her just in case.

In spite of his frustration, Willie smiled as he watched Katy climb the ladder and slide into the pit of colorful balls. She was having fun, even if he wasn't. Sometimes she played with the other kids; other times she ignored them and played by herself, hiding under the balls and then struggling to climb out of the pit and up the ladder to slide again.

A couple of loud boys entered the playroom and noisily took over the slide. Willie guessed they were about thirteen or fourteen—too old for the playroom. Most of the other kids moved out of their way or left, but not Katy. Willie stood up and moved closer to the window, concerned that they might scare or intimidate her. But she just smiled at them and continued taking her turn on the slide.

Tired of this hypervigilance and wanting to spend time with Katy, Willie decided it was time to leave. He leaned his head in the door and caught Katy's attention. "Two more minutes to play," he shouted over the echoing noise of kids at play. He smiled as he watched her attack her recreation with renewed vigor and determination not to waste a single precious moment.

He waited about a minute and then signaled her to come.

"Daddy," she said, breathless from running. "Did you see me do a somersault? Did you see?"

"Yes, you were great!" Willie assured her as he helped her put on her coat and mittens.

"Do we hafta go home already, Daddy?"

Willie was asking himself the same question. "Why don't we go for a little ride and look at the Christmas lights," he suggested.

"Yay!" Katy shouted. "We get to ride in Daddy's truck and see the pretty Christmas lights! Let's go!"

Willie always got a kick out of Katy's enthusiasm for his truck. They never went anywhere in Dad's truck as a family. Bekah hated riding in it; it rode rough and was always dirty. But Katy loved it. Willie suspected it was because she could throw her trash on the floor. Bekah had suggested that the truck was big and strong like Willie and made Katy feel like she was part of her daddy's world. Whatever the reason, Katy liked it, and Willie liked her being there.

He took her to the passenger side and carefully buckled her into her car seat. "Now don't mess anything up," Willie teased her before closing the door and walking around to the driver's side. "You know I just cleaned this ol' truck up last year." Katy giggled.

When he started the car, his CD player roared to life with a familiar tune. Katy wrinkled up her little nose and pronounced judgment. "Not that one, Daddy. Play Christmas songs."

"You're sure you wouldn't rather listen to Tim McGraw or Kenny Chesney?" he asked. He knew he would, but she shook her curly mop adamantly.

"Christmas."

He popped in his one Christmas CD and pushed Play. "I'm dreaming of a white Christmas . . ."

They listened for a while in silence, broken only by Katy's appreciative exclamations whenever they spotted even the most humble lighting display.

As they drove down a peaceful country road with no Christmas lights, Katy slipped her little hand into his. "Thanks for letting me play, Dad," she told him. "I had lots of fun."

"Katy," Willie asked her thoughtfully, "wasn't it too crowded and noisy?"

"Oh no, it's fun having lots of people to play with. And when it's noisy, you can hear all the fun everybody's having."

"How about when those big boys came in. Didn't they scare you?"

Katy shook her head no.

"Why not?"

"'Cuz I knew you were watching me, and my Dad is bigger and stronger than anyone. Hey, Dad, this is a good one. Turn it up!"

She pointed her mittened hand toward the CD player, and he dutifully obeyed.

"Silent night, holy night; all is calm, all is bright . . ."

His mind wandered back to Katy's words, but not for long.

"Listen!" Katy insisted.

"Sleep in heavenly peace, sleep in heavenly peace."

"Play it again," she begged. He pushed the button and started it all over again. "Silent night . . ."

He listened, this time hearing the words as if for the first time. Looking over, he saw that in spite of the bumps and jolts of his old truck, Katy was slumped down in her seat, peacefully sleeping.

Suddenly it all fit together perfectly. The dark, peaceful road, the silence of the night, his little girl's words and example of trust and rest. He knew in his heart that he'd been wasting his time and energy worrying and being resentful about the situation he was in. He couldn't change it, but he could make the best of it and find joy and purpose where he could. Besides, suddenly he felt the peaceful assurance that his strong, powerful heavenly Father knew where he was and was watching him.

Willie pushed the button to play the song again. "Silent night, holy night; all is calm, all is bright." The stars above had never seemed brighter to Willie. For the first time in a long time, Willie knew that tonight he would sleep in heavenly peace.

Chapter Seven

Treasure

Chapter Seven

Treasure

You are My masterpiece
in progress. No matter what
mistakes you make, you can
be confident I'll complete the
good work I've started in you.
When you feel stress getting
the best of you, I won't let you
be crushed. When you don't
understand your circumstances,
I won't let you despair. When
you fall, you won't be destroyed.
Through all your trials, I'll
never abandon you.

TREASURING YOU,

Your Heavenly Father

—from Philippians 1:6; 2 Corinthians 4:8–9; Hebrews 13:5

Being Dad to a daughter isn't always easy, but it's always, always worth it. The truth is, daughters scare their dads a little bit. They're so delicate and fragile, and it doesn't take long for Dad to realize that he knows how to throw a football but not a tea party. As Daddy's little girl navigates through the confusing waters of first love and tempestuous emotions, daughters often seem incredibly complicated to their simple dads.

I may not always understand you, but I always, always love you. You are my treasure, like a gemstone of great beauty and unequalled worth. Maybe I don't always communicate that to you adequately. Sometimes you still surprise me; circumstances catch me off guard. It often takes me a while to think things through and know what I feel and what I want to say to you. Sometimes I react without thinking. I've said some foolish, hurtful things at those times—things that I later regret. Please forgive my shortcomings. But always remember: nothing you do—or anything I say—will ever change how much I love you. It's just not possible to shake the deep, abiding love I have for you, my daughter.

You are my precious treasure—you have been since the day you were born and will continue to be until the day I die. Don't ever let anyone make you doubt your worth. Your father knows the truth: you are a great treasure.

There's something like a line of gold thread running through a man's words when he talks to his daughter, and gradually over the years it gets to be long enough for you to pick up in your hands and weave into a cloth that feels like love itself.

John Gregory Brown

Lindsey dreaded facing her dad. Would he be red-faced with anger, or would he have that pitiful disappointed look that made her feel like such a failure?

Love Letters

The whole house seemed to shake as Randy Wilson slammed the door and hurriedly left the house. He was angry, and he didn't care who knew it. He and his daughter, Lindsey, had argued yet again, and he just wanted to get out of there. Reaching into his pocket and finding his keys, he quickly unlocked his car and slid into the driver's seat. As he fumbled with the keys, trying to start the engine, he slapped the dash with his other hand.

"Why?" His shout came out like an agonized roar. His normally peaceful home had become a place of turmoil. It seemed he and Lindsey were always arguing. Why was this happening? Why?

Randy took pride in being a good dad. He had determined years ago that being a dad was going to be his top priority, and he thought he was a pretty good parent. He and Lindsey had always enjoyed a good relationship. Lindsey called herself a daddy's girl, which of course made Randy extremely proud. But something had changed over the course of the last few months.

Lindsey had turned sixteen, and the sudden changes in her behavior had caught Randy off guard. For the first time, he couldn't seem to get through to her. He was frustrated.

And now this. Last night his wife, Cindy, had shown him something she'd found in Lindsey's pocket while doing laundry. It was a love letter to Lindsey from a boy named André—a letter that shocked Randy and Cindy and made them blush.

When Randy had confronted Lindsey with the letter this morning, her pale look of horror had quickly transformed into red-faced rage. Suddenly he was the bad guy for invading her privacy. How had things managed to get twisted around so completely?

Driving across town to his office, Randy's anger slowly melted into empty sadness. His stomach felt twisted in a big knot. Guilt gnawed at him for leaving home in such anger. His mind raced wildly. How involved was Lindsey with this sex-crazed boy? What was happening to his family? Was he losing his little girl? Where had he gone wrong? Why couldn't Lindsey just listen to him and do what she was supposed to do? Would he ever have a happy family again? Then he remembered the last thing he'd said to Lindsey before storming out of the house. "I'll love you forever, Lindsey, but right now I don't like you very much."

Lindsey drove to her high school in sullen anger. The nerve of him! What right did he have to go through her personal belongings? Maybe Nikki and Hailey were right: parents never trust you—and you can never trust parents! They obviously still thought of her as a child. Didn't they see how adult she was becoming? André did.

The thought of André brought a sudden flush of shame. She desperately wished her mom and dad hadn't read the suggestive note he had written to her. André was really hot. Almost every girl in school would be flattered by his attention. And she was, but he was also making her uncomfortable—big time. She wanted him to talk with her, ask her out for pizza, and think she was fascinating and appealing. He obviously wanted something else. She didn't like to think of herself the way André apparently did. Didn't he recognize that what really made her valuable was who she was as a person? She didn't think he did.

Still, they looked awfully good together, and his interest was doing wonders for her popularity. Until this year Nikki and Hailey and the other popular girls had seemed way out of her league. This year they had drawn her into their circle. But her membership in their clique still seemed tenuous at times, and she needed to be careful not to do something that would precipitate her fall from the in group. Getting dumped by André would definitely be that something.

I can't believe Dad told me he didn't like me very much right now. The words still stung. *What's happened to us? Why can't he understand me and recognize that I'm growing up? Why doesn't he trust me?* Her dad had always been strict. He made rules and expected his children to respect and obey them. Disobedience brought discipline—something her younger brother, John, had felt often, but Lindsey rarely. Until now, that is. Just as she was starting to be mature enough to make her own decisions, her dad seemed to be getting stricter and making more rules. All she wanted was a little independence, but it seemed more and more that her dad wanted to control her life.

She parked her car and checked her makeup in the mirror. When she was reasonably sure no one would notice she'd been crying, she got out and headed toward the school building. Hailey and Nikki waved to her from the front stairs and waited for her to catch up.

"Dad, I haven't done anything wrong. I can't control what André wrote that he feels about me, but that's not how I think of him. If you trusted me, you'd know that—or at least you'd have asked me and not assumed."

Her dad was silent for a moment. Then he gently put his arm around her shoulder, gave her a little squeeze, and spoke softly. "Maybe you're right. If you say you haven't done anything inappropriate, I believe you. Honey, I love you. I just want what's best for you. But even if you haven't done anything to get in trouble, I'm very concerned about the way your attitude has changed. You've been disrespectful to your mother and me, and we don't feel that you're being totally honest with us. Quite frankly, some of your new friends don't seem to be a very good influence."

"Dad!" Lindsey protested. "What's wrong with my friends? Why don't you like them?"

"It's not that I don't like them. I just worry that they don't have the same values we do and that they could influence you to make bad decisions."

"Dad, don't you trust me?"

"I want to trust you, but that doesn't mean I trust your friends. I don't know them very well, but it seems they've already changed you some."

"Of course I'm changing, Dad," Lindsey said, exasperated. "I'm growing up. I can't stay your little girl forever."

"You'll always be my little girl," Randy said firmly. "And I'm not trying to keep you from growing up. I want you to grow up. Just don't spend so much time trying to please your friends that you fail to please yourself—or God. These friends may not even be part of your life in a few years; but you'll still be living with the choices you make now." He kissed her forehead, lingered for a moment, then whispered in her ear. "You're a treasure, Lindsey Wilson. Guard the treasure."

The next day at school Lindsey found another love letter tucked in her lunch bag. This one was from her dad.

> *Lindsey,*
>   *I'm sorry things have been strained between us lately. I'll do my best to trust you. I ask only that you be honest with Mom and me. We love you and want what's best for you.*
>   *Love, Dad*

"How lame," Nikki said, reading the note over Lindsey's shoulder. "Parents always say they want what's good for you, but they're just doing what's good for them."

Lindsey covered the note self-consciously so no one else would read it. "Yeah, lame." She tried to match Nikki's dismissive tone as she shoved the note into her purse. "Probably just a momentary twinge of guilt for yelling at me."

"Save that for your scrapbook," Hailey added sarcastically. "Parents rarely apologize—and their nice words never last long."

But they did, Lindsey found.

Every day, for an entire semester, Lindsey found another loving note from her dad. When she was taking exams, he encouraged her, writing that he was praying she'd do her best.

When her basketball team went to an out-of-town weekend tournament, he wrote that he'd miss her but would drive the family over to cheer for her. When they'd had an argument, he always wrote that it didn't change how much he loved her. The day she went to the prom with André, her dad reminded her that she was a treasure—and that she shouldn't tolerate anyone treating her as anything less.

Lindsey shoved that latest note into her purse and quickly forgot about it. She had so much to do to get ready for tonight. André would be picking her up in seven hours, and she wanted to look stunning. She could hardly wait to be dancing in the arms of the man who loved her.

Lindsey stood in the rain outside Hailey's house, crying. Her beautiful dress and hair were a mess, and she was sure her makeup was running down her face with the tears and rain. She was so glad to be out of that place. Prom had been like a wonderful, magical dream. But when Lindsey had decided to deliberately break curfew to go to a big party after the prom, everything had gone bad. She'd been miserable at the party. Alcohol was abundant, and it seemed everyone was doing things Lindsey knew were wrong. André was the worst. The way he looked at her, his language, the way he pressured her—she didn't want to be with him. Didn't even want him to take her home.

She didn't know what else to do, so she called home. She could hear the stress in her father's voice when he answered. Much to Lindsey's relief, he didn't say much but promised to come right away.

Now out of the scary environment of the party, for the first time Lindsey felt the danger of waiting alone outside after midnight and hoped her dad would get there soon. He was going to kill her, but at least she'd live. Although right now Dad was the best of three evils, she still dreaded facing him. Would he be red-faced with anger, or would he have that pitiful disappointed look that made her feel like such a failure?

She saw headlights but hung back, not wanting to approach a stranger's car. Before she could even be certain, the car squealed to a stop, the door flew open, and her dad ran toward her. She looked into his face, anxious to know his mood. What she saw made her jaw drop and pricked her heart. Not anger, not disappointment— Lindsey saw true fear in her dad's eyes. He was worried about her. He took her in his arms and hugged her tightly.

"Oh, Lindsey, are you all right?"

She nodded and noticed her makeup smeared on his coat.

"I'm so glad you called me. Thank you."

He steered her toward the car, never once relaxing his grip on her. For the first time she realized that it wasn't a confining grip, but an embrace of love. She was warmed and awed by the depth and power of that love. Yes, she finally was in the arms of the man who loved her—and it felt wonderful.